I'm Reading About

MASSACHUSETTS

The Bay State!

GALLOPADE

by Carole Marsh

Printed and Manufactured in Peachtree City, GA., USA
www.gallopade.com

Book design: John Hanson

Editorial manager: Janice Baker

Massachusetts is a great state.

It is one of a kind.

What makes Massachusetts special?

Let's read about it and see!

NATIVE AMERICANS

Who lived in Massachusetts first?

Native Americans did!

They moved around to find food.
They hunted in Massachusetts' woods.
They fished in Massachusetts' rivers.
They gathered fruits and seeds and nuts.

EXPLORERS

Some of the first explorers to Massachusetts arrived in 1497–98. They came from the country of England.

John Cabot was their leader. He and his men sailed along the Massachusetts coast.

SETTLEMENT

A group of people known as the Pilgrims
came from England to America.
They started the first settlement in Massachusetts.
They named it Plymouth.

The Pilgrims wanted freedom to worship
as they pleased!

Massachusetts was one
of the original
13 colonies.

Plymouth

STATEHOOD

Massachusetts was the sixth state
to join the United States of America!

Isn't it great,
to be a state!
I bet Massachusetts
could hardly wait!

Massachusetts became a state in 1788.

Massachusetts
The 6th State

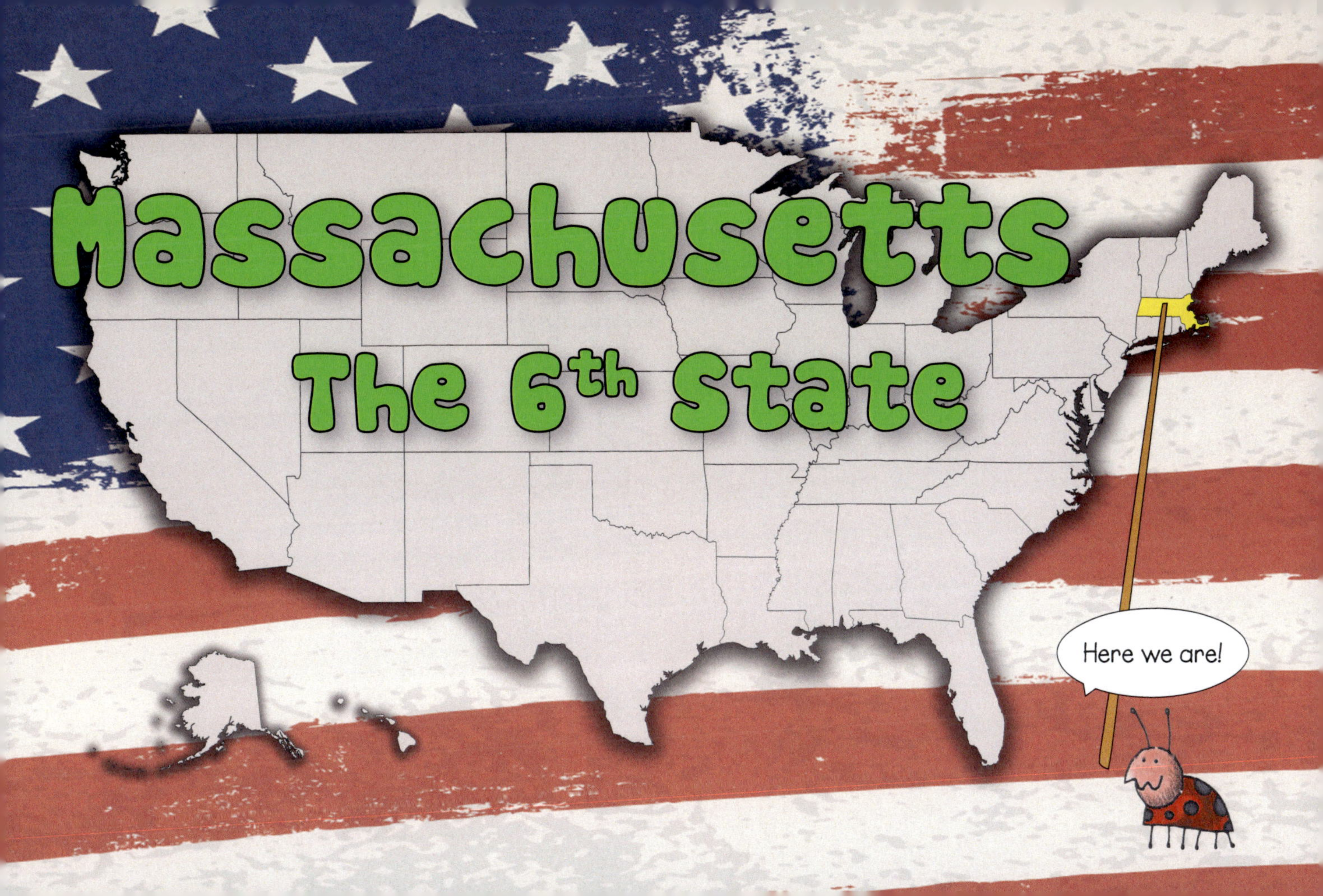

FLAG

I am the state flag.

What color am I?
I am white.

Look at me.
What else do you see?

I fly high over the state of Massachusetts!

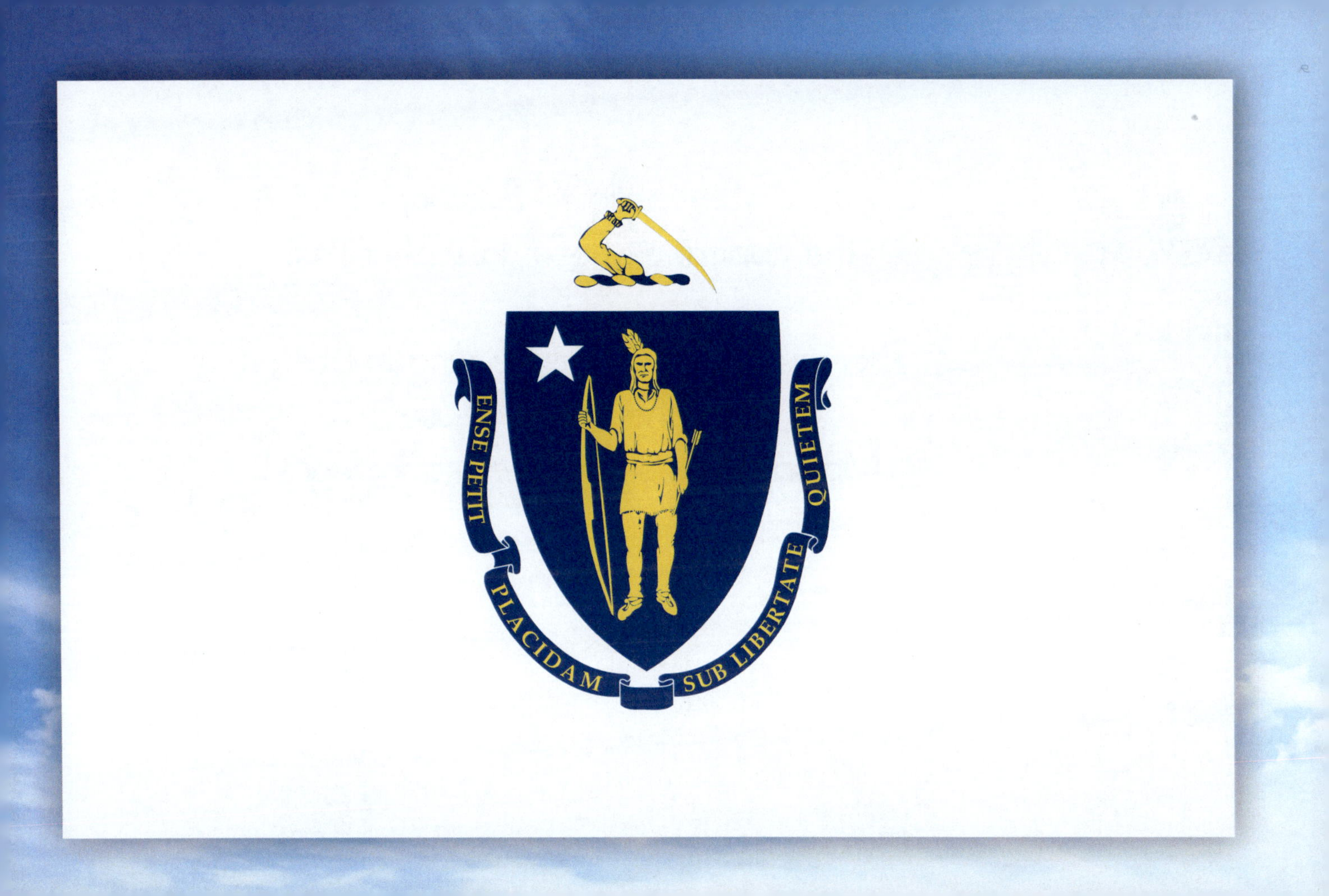
ENSE PETIT
PLACIDAM
SUB LIBERTATE
QUIETEM

CAPITAL

Say hello to Boston,
the capital city of Massachusetts!

There is an important building in Boston.
It is the State House.
Massachusetts laws are made there!

State House
Boston
Capital

SEAL

I am a seal,
but I am not the State Seal.
If I were, I would be very important.
I would be stamped on many official papers.
(Ouch, that might hurt!)

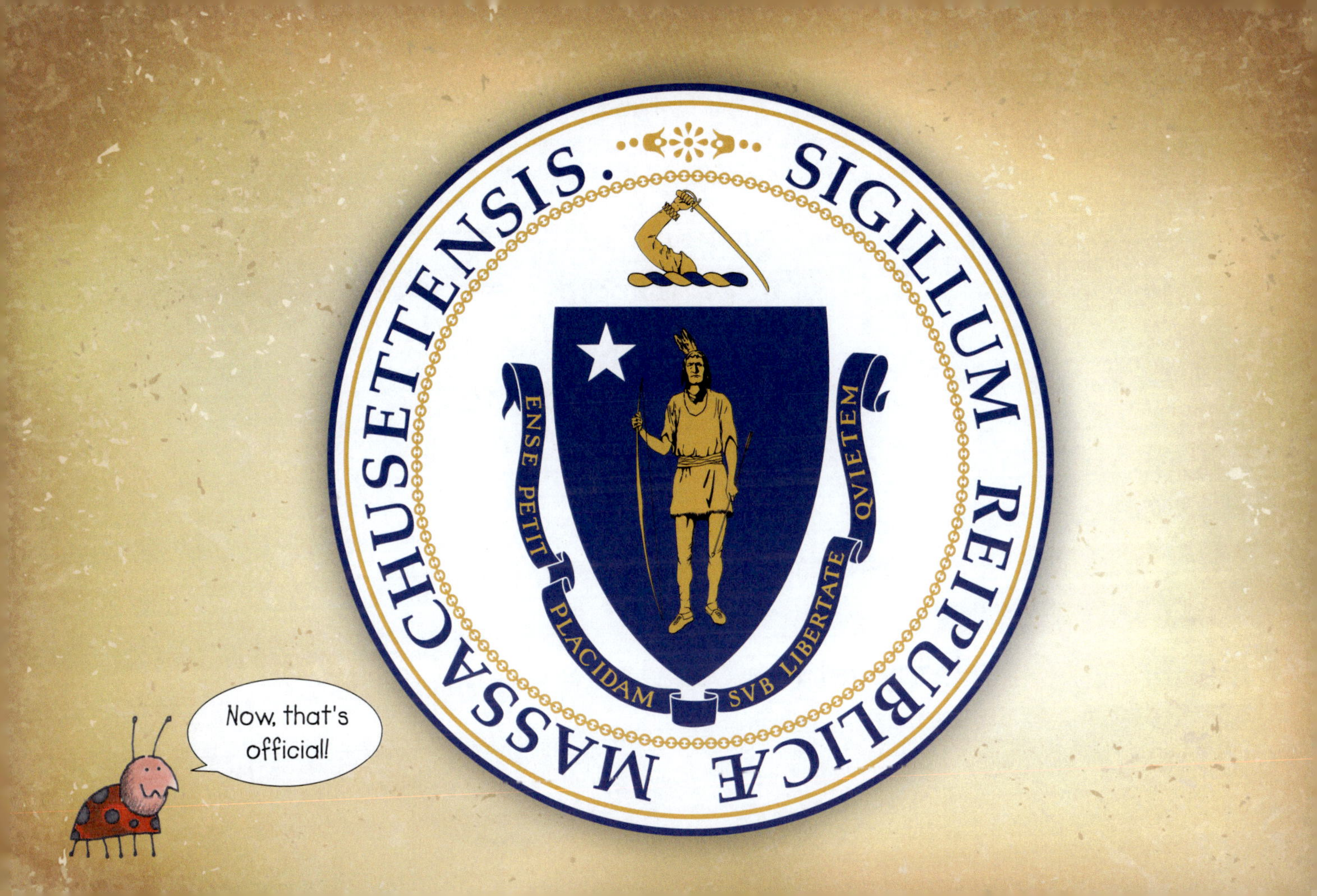
SIGILLUM REIPUBLICÆ MASSACHUSETTENSIS.
ENSE PETIT PLACIDAM SVB LIBERTATE QVIETEM
Now, that's official!

NICKNAME

State nicknames are fun!
State nicknames are great!
They share fun facts
about each state!

Massachusetts's nickname is "The Bay State."

Early settlers built towns along Cape Cod Bay!

Borders

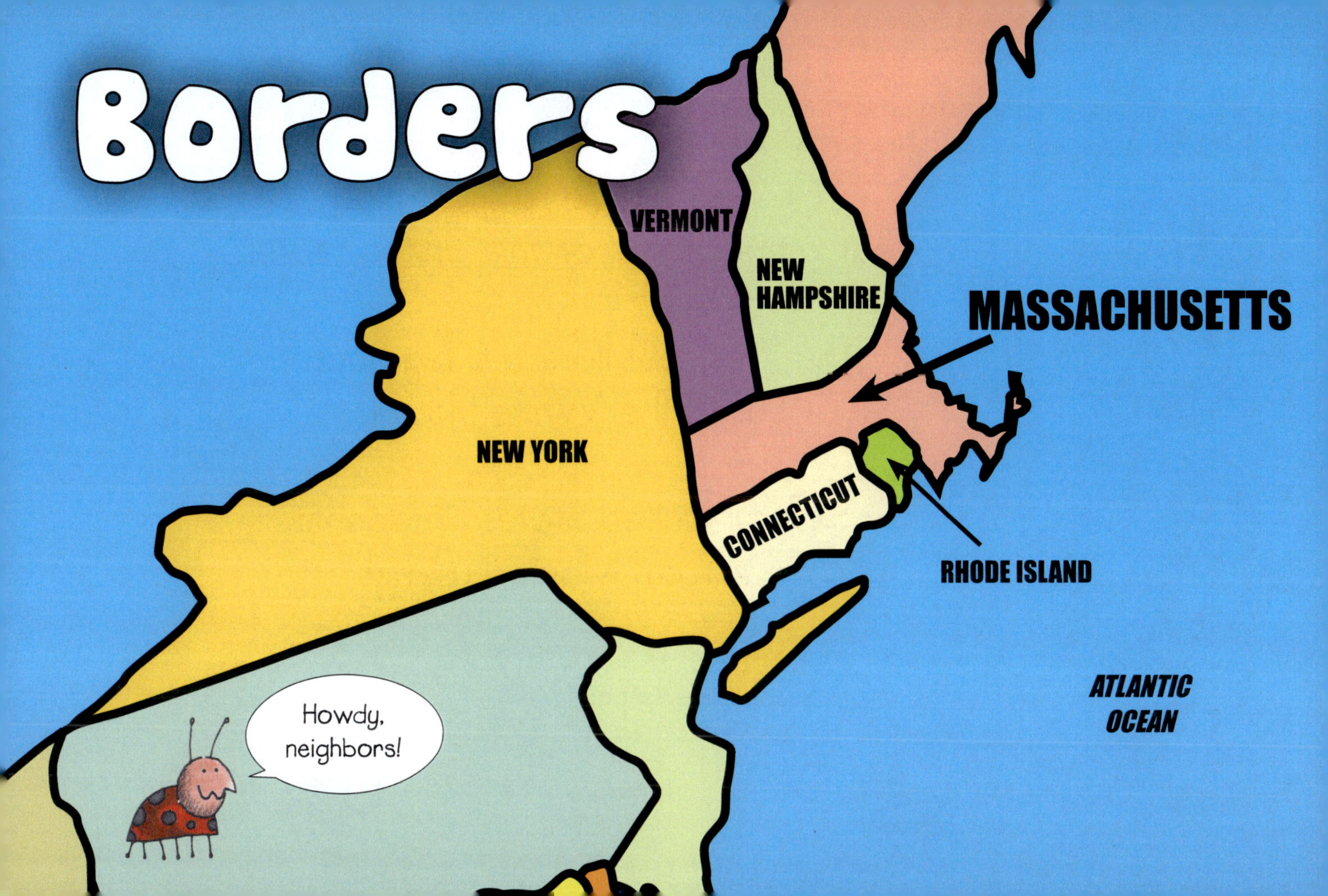
VERMONT
NEW HAMPSHIRE
MASSACHUSETTS
NEW YORK
CONNECTICUT
RHODE ISLAND
ATLANTIC OCEAN
Howdy, neighbors!

PRESIDENT

The President is the leader of our country.
He lives in Washington, D.C.
That is the capital of the United States.

The President lives in a big house
called the White House.

Several United States Presidents
are from Massachusetts!

John Adams
2nd President
John Quincy Adams
6th President
Calvin Coolidge
30th President
John F. Kennedy
35th President
George H.W. Bush
41st President

PEOPLE

Many famous people

Benjamin Franklin

One of the Founding Fathers of the United States

Eli Whitney

Invented the cotton gin that separated seeds from cotton

Susan B. Anthony

Helped women gain the right to vote

call our state home!

Clara Barton
Founded the American Red Cross

W.E.B. Du Bois
Worked for equal rights for African Americans

Theodore Geisel
Children's book writer known as "Dr. Seuss"

PEOPLE

Black-Capped Chickadee

BIRD

I am the state bird, and I fly
over Massachusetts, proud and high.

As I fly, up in the sky,
I flap my wings to tell you "Hi!"

The Massachusetts state bird is the
Black-Capped Chickadee.

Mayflower

FLOWER

I am the Mayflower.
I am the state flower.

I like to grow in partly shady areas.
I bloom in spring and summer.
I help make Massachusetts beautiful!

Look at me! Smell me!
My blooms have five petals.

American Elm

TREE

I am an American Elm—I'm the state tree.
All over Massachusetts is where to find me.

My roots run deep, they keep me strong.
I can live for hundreds of years—that's very long!

I stand up straight, big and tall.
Don't climb too high—it would hurt to fall!

Ladybug

INSECT

I am the Ladybug
I am the state insect.

I am a type of beetle.
I am red with black polka dots!

Gardeners and farmers love me.
I eat bugs off their plants.
I help Massachusetts crops grow.

Atlantic Ocean

Let's go to the beach!

We can swim in the waves.
We can play in the sand.

We can build a big castle
where water meets land.

Massachusetts' beaches are home to many animals:

Sea Turtles **Fish** **Birds** **Crabs** **Dolphins** **and More!**

BEACHES

Mountains

MOUNTAINS

Massachusetts' mountains are the place to be.
Hiking and camping—
fun for you and me.

Winter weather brings lots of snow.
Temperatures drop to freezing and below!

Hockomock Swamp

SWAMPS

The Hockomock Swamp is in southeastern Massachusetts.
The swamp provides a natural barrier against floods.

This habitat is home to many animals:

Birds **Deer** **Snakes** **Frogs** **and More!**

The Wampanoag Indians used to hide in the swamp.
There, they launched attacks against the white settlers!

Plymouth Rock

LANDMARK

Plymouth Rock is a special rock!
The Pilgrims landed at Plymouth Rock
when they came to America.
They traveled on a ship called the *Mayflower*.

Visitors to Massachusetts can visit Plymouth Rock.
It is a memorial to the Pilgrims' voyage!

The date "1620" is carved into Plymouth Rock.
That is the year the Pilgrims arrived!

Massachusetts Crops

Massachusetts has many farms.
Why?
Because Massachusetts has good soil and
a mild climate!

Some of the top crops grown in Massachusetts are:

Cranberries **Hay** **Apples** **Corn**

Sports in Massachusetts

SPORTS

Baseball! Basketball! Hockey! Football!
Massachusetts has it all.

Whether you like to watch or play,
You are sure to have a ball!

Bruins **Celtics** **Red Sox**

Patriots

Eagles

Minutemen **& More!**

Massachusetts: Home of the Boston Tea Party

CLAIM TO FAME

The Boston Tea Party took place
in Boston Harbor in 1773.

But this tea party wasn't really a party.
A group of colonists dressed as Indians
threw boxes of tea into the harbor.
They were protesting British taxes!

The colonists dumped 342 chests
of tea into the water.
It took them about three
hours to do it!

GLOSSARY

climate: weather conditions in an area over a long period of time

colony: a settlement ruled by another country

elect: to choose someone by voting

habitat: a place where plants or animals naturally live

laws: rules made by the government

memorial: something designed to preserve the memory of a person or event

region: an area that has similar characteristics

settlement: the first community in an area

swamp: a low area of land that is often partly covered with water

taxes: fees charged by the government